BURMA

EVERGREEN is an imprint of Benedikt Taschen Verlag GmbH

© for this edition: 1998 Benedikt Taschen Verlag GmbH
Hohenzollernring 53, D-50672 Köln
© 1997 Editions du Chêne – Hachette Livre – La Birmanie
Under the direction of Michel Buntz – Hoa Qui Photographic Agency
Editor: Corinne Fossey
Map and illustrations: Jean-Michel Kirsch
Text: Jean-Yves Montagu
Photographs: Jean-Léo Dugast/Hoa-Qui (except pages 48-49 and 51 B. Perousse, and pages 108-109 C. Boisvieux)
Cover design: Angelika Taschen, Cologne
Translated by Alayne Pullen
In association with First Edition Translations Ltd, Cambridge
Realization of the English edition by First Edition Translations Ltd, Cambridge

Printed in Italy
ISBN 3-8228-7644-5
GB

BURMA

Text JEAN-YVES MONTAGU
Photographs JEAN-LÉO DUGAST

EVERGREEN

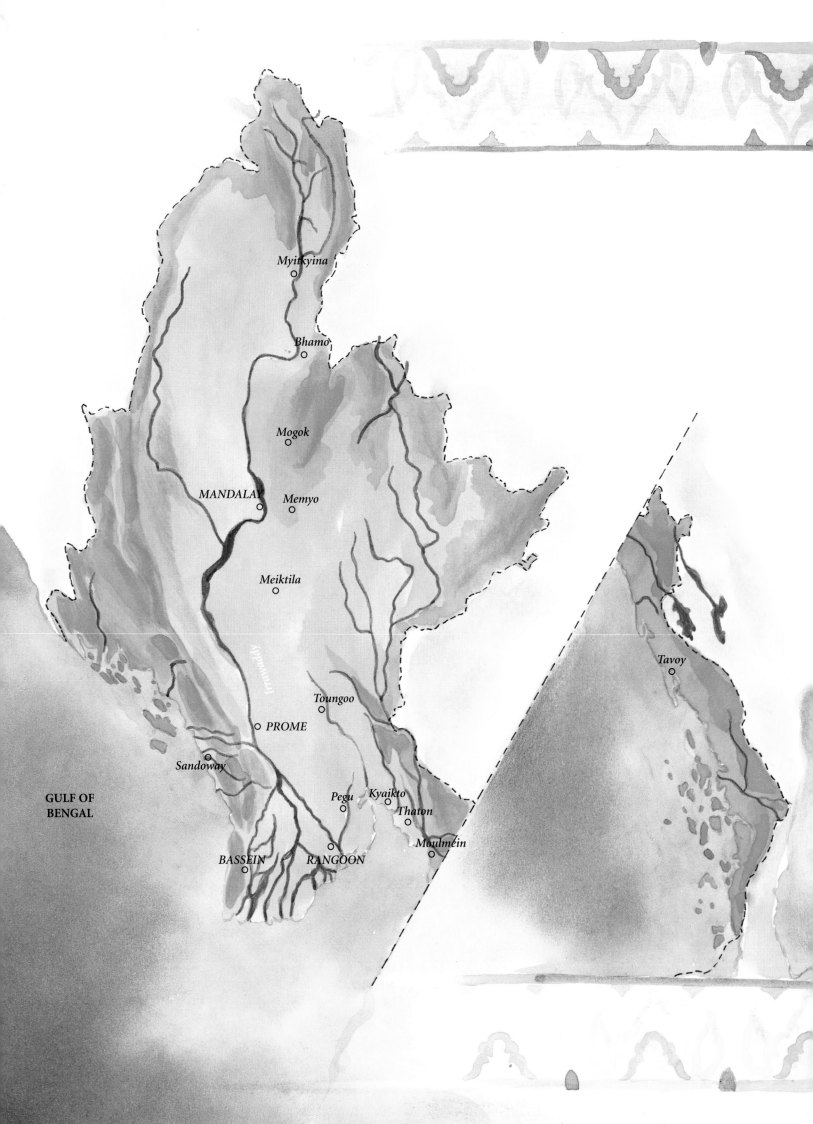

Myitkyina

Bhamo

Mogok

MANDALAY   *Memyo*

Meiktila

Irrawaddy

Toungoo

PROME

Sandoway

GULF OF
BENGAL

Pegu   *Kyaikto*

Thaton

Moulmein

BASSEIN   RANGOON

Tavoy

Then, a golden mystery upheaved itself on the horizon – a beautiful winking wonder that blazed in the sun, of a shape that was neither Muslim dome nor Hindu spire. ... 'There's the old Shway Dagon,' said my companion. ... The golden dome said: 'This is Burma, and it will be quite unlike any land you know about.'

Rudyard Kipling, *From Sea to Sea and other Sketches (1904).*

Climbing upwards, the path takes a sudden, sharp bend to aid the ascent. In places tree trunks have been thrown across gullies and straddle waterfalls. As I move onwards, the silence grows to a murmur – calm yet powerful like a river, with distant sounds audible from its banks.

I can see the top of the ravine sparkling in the silver light of the river. Before long the rising moon will slip between the branches of the trees. All about me a rustling begins, rising upwards, stirring the leaves and receding before the spectacle of night.

Each evening night comes to Burma like a wakening giant – a powerful sorcerer transforming the theatre of shadows into a puppet theatre. Those entertainments are known here as *yok thei pwe*. Yesterday evening I watched one in a local village; it had twenty-eight characters, some of whom were as much as 1 metre [over 3 ft] tall. These entertainments last three nights, but the set remains the same: a white cotton backdrop with a throne to the left and a divan in the centre. All of fate is symbolised here, from power to mystery; all desire is expressed in the simple figures of twenty-eight puppets, among them Thagyamin, king of the *nat**.

From the air Burma resembles a giant kite. In the extreme north of this diamond-shaped land lie the Kachin Hills – massifs of primary rock cut through by deep valleys. The Shan Plateau to the east is formed by two flat plains sloping eastwards. To the west are the Arakan range and the Chin Hills extending the outer rim of the Indian archipelago, with the Tenasserim (Taninthuryi) archipelago forming the long, narrow tail of the country. This long north–south 'spine' to Burma, though not particularly high, includes the pass of

* A *nat* is a spirit in the Burmese animist pantheon.

the Three Pagodas, through which the famous Kwai valley in Thailand can be reached.

The string of this giant kite is the sparkling Irrawaddy river, which rises in the southern Himalayas and runs for 2,710 km [1,680 miles] through Burma from north to south before dividing and flowing through its branching delta into the Andaman Sea – a delta with nine branches like the nine feathers of the parrot that hides among the lotus flowers.

As I write, I am travelling by boat towards one of these branches of the river delta. The sound of the waves is beginning to subside. I feel an increasing appreciation of the interplay of physical and metaphysical relations – of how a person open to the revelation of divine light will comprehend as much truth as the bee may garner nectar on its flight between the flowers and its hive. This secret truth, communicated through the interplay of form, is expressed in the Vedas – the sacred Hindu texts. The message is the fundamental law of life. If people are capable of achieving wisdom through intuition, a new dimension will open before them.

In 1989 Burma was given the new name of Myanmar. In semantic terms this represents a return to the roots of the country's age-old culture: Myanmar was the name Marco Polo gave the country in his account of his travels in the thirteenth century. In terms of democracy, however, things are more complicated.

Throughout its history waves of different peoples have entered Myanmar and intermixed, forming a population whose distribution has been determined by the country's geography. The Mon, who arrived perhaps as early as 3000 BC, belong to the Khmer peoples of Cambodia. They brought with them an Indian culture, the cult of Vishnu, and Buddhism. In early Christian times the Pyu (a Tibeto-Burman race) moved into the Irrawaddy valley, and in about 850 the Burmese – having assimilated the Pyu – occupied the rich farming areas and founded the kingdom of Pagan (Bagan). Siam (present-day Thailand) benefited from the decline of this kingdom, which originated in the thirteenth century, and between

1530 and 1780 Burmese hegemony and Siamese domination alternated, before disappearing – in Burma's case – under British rule. In 1885 the British took control of Burma. In 1942 the Japanese invaded, granting the country independence in principle in 1943. A long period of unrest ensued, ending on 2 March 1962 with a coup d'état which placed General Ne Win in power. He was replaced in 1988 by a military junta known as SLORC (State Law and Order Restoration Council).

Myanmar occupies an area of 677,000 sq km [262,000 sq miles] and is situated between Thailand and Laos to the east, Bangladesh to the west, and China and India to the north. It lies between 20 degrees north and 10 degrees south and has an estimated population of 44 million, of which 75 per cent live in rural areas. The tropic of cancer runs through the country north of Mogok in the Mandalay division and passes through the Chin, Kachin, and Shan states.

Myanmar is a federal republic consisting of the seven 'divisions' that make up Burma itself and seven states inhabited by non-Burmese peoples. This mixture of peoples and languages has created a kind of Asiatic Babel which some have compared to a parrot. Facing westwards its beak touches Sittwe (Akyab), its claws enclose Yangon (Rangoon), its tail stretches down the Tanintharyi (Tenasserim) peninsula, while its unfolded wings form the country's three northern states. At its longest, from north to south, Myanmar is approximately 2,000 km [1,242 miles] in length, and at its widest, from east to west, some 1,000 km [620 miles] wide.

Some evenings wise old men in the villages of Myanmar will talk of this vast land. I like to sit by them as the day draws to a close. Gradually the familiar words and events of the west fade away. Like the golden wings of a magnificent bird passing by, the sunset spreads across the sky, transforming the universe in dazzling silence. For a few seconds only you can see quite clearly how it seeks its nest, and your being beckons it home. Night opens out to claim it like the hands of the giant that wakens here each evening – the sorcerer casting his spell over the magic that is Burma.

Many examples of colonial architecture can still be found in the centre of Rangoon.
Opposite:
The red-brick building of the High Court of Justice is one.

At first sight the old colonial buildings still standing in Rangoon as a legacy of the British Empire are reminiscent of red-brick potteries hidden among the branches of the palm trees – though the decorative gilding on the façade of the Victorian Court House suggests some secret alphabet derived from ancient Burmese mythology.

The city of Rangoon, or Yangon as it is now known, was built on the site of the ancient city of Dagon, which means 'the end of strife'. When the cocktail hour arrives, peace does indeed come to this ancient place. In the bar of the Strand Hotel the gentle music of a Burmese harp spills its notes into the air like sequins of sound falling among the bridge players. Then, lifted on the breeze of the fan, they seem to descend again, ceremonially, like confetti – traces of a long-gone empire, scattered by the wind.

It was in 1824 that the Anglo-Indian expeditionary force landed in Dagon. The reasons for its arrival were twofold: state security and also the need to demonstrate solidarity in matters of formal etiquette. The Rajah of Manipur (a state in eastern Assam) had

Over the years many of the city's buildings have been left to decay. Their present state does little justice to the interesting ornamentation they display.

refused to attend the coronation of the king of Burma, and the Burmese king therefore felt compelled to despatch an expeditionary force against him. The mistake the new monarch made was to believe that the English would remain indifferent to a military deployment taking place on the very threshold of their Indian possessions. It was later claimed by the more cynical that Britain had simply been waiting for an opportunity that would allow her to descend on Rangoon.

British domination of Burma took place in two phases. Twenty-eight years after the first landing the British followed up with a second, embarking on a partitioning operation so successful that on 1 January 1886 Burma became a province of the Indian Empire. The British took over all the administrative posts although, in the border areas where minority groups predominated, local chiefs acted as intermediaries for the colonial power.

The British displayed a preference for drawing the armed forces from among the mountain tribes of the north and for using Indian auxiliaries. This wounded national pride and led to tension in the

country. Nevertheless, the British presence saw the start of genuine economic progress in Burma, especially in the Irrawaddy delta. Those who benefited most from this were the English firms controlling the wholesale trade and their various satellites – mainly Indian and Chinese retailers. However, the pawnbrokers flourished too, leading the peasant farmers into ever greater debt and eventually reducing them to the rank of agricultural workers. By 1890 anti-British feeling had begun to develop. At the end of the First World War India acquired a certain degree of autonomy, but it was not until 1923 that Burma followed suit.

The year 1934 saw the start of an independence movement led by the association known as 'We the Burmese', but this soon fell prey to the designs of the Japanese, who saw Burma as a Trojan horse capable of helping them achieve their imperialist ambitions. With the support of Aung San's Burmese liberation army, the Japanese invaded the country from Thailand, notably via the Three Pagodas Pass, driving the British out of Rangoon in March 1942. A long period of political and military confusion ensued between the

Making your way along the city's pavements can be difficult – they are lined with stalls selling fruit, vegetables, and flowers.

British, the Japanese, the Nationalists, and also the Americans, who were fighting both Japanese expansionism and the danger posed by communist China.

In August 1942 the victorious Japanese, who now controlled the country, installed a national government and recognised Burmese independence. However, the abuses perpetrated by the Japanese powers caused such discontent among the population that the Nationalists turned once again to the Allied powers. In March 1945 the Burmese national army called for a general revolt. On 3 May 1945, with the military support of the British and American forces, Rangoon was retaken.

Burmese food is similar to that of India and makes use of many different spices. This market stall shows the range available.

After the war the British moved back into Burma with promises of a political settlement. However, these promises were slow to materialise, and this led to a general strike and violent disturbances in the country. Finally, on 4 January 1948, Burma proclaimed its independence and left the Commonwealth.

The early years of the new republic were marked by a series of coups d'état and assassinations within the council of ministers. The nationalist leader Aung San (father of Aung San Suu Kyi – the present leader of the National League for Democracy) and six other ministers were assassinated. The government had a succession of different leaders: U Nu, Ne Win, Sein Lwin, Maung Maung, and Saw Maung – who, in September 1988, installed a military regime. He was replaced in April 1992 by General Than Shwe.

With a little luck it is still possible to meet some of the rare survivors of the Second World War. One evening in the Strand Hotel bar I came across Walter. He had served in General Orde Charles Wingate's Chindits before going into the import–export business. The Chindits were the British, Indian, Chin, Kachin, and Gurkha soldiers who

drove the rear of the Japanese troops out of Burma. Their name is a reference to the Chinthé, the half-lion half-griffon creature of Burmese mythology appointed as guardian of the pagodas.

These men had taken part in the construction of the famous Ledo Road together with 35,000 other British, Burmese, Chinese, and Indian soldiers. So many died during the course of the construction that it became known as the 'man a mile' road. When the 800 km [500 mile] road finally opened in May 1945, the war was almost over. Today ivy covers the track as it fades back into the jungle and into the realms of myth while the greying façades of the old colonial buildings stand like veteran guards gazing unblinkingly into eternity.

When the sun carves its breathtaking spirals among the clouds, unleashing downpours of apocalyptic proportions, that is when the magic of Rangoon begins. It is as if a multitude of spirits are descending, each crystallised within a drop of water and illuminating the rooftops in a ridge of sparkling light. Rangoon is more than just a city; it is a luxuriant revitalising force constantly replenished like the fruit displayed on its market stalls.

At sunrise the streets of the capital come alive. Here women are buying sprigs of jasmine to decorate their hair.

The markets of Rangoon are numerous and varied. Colour and fragrance abound with arrays of spices and medicinal plants for which miraculous properties are claimed. At the snake market it is possible to buy the fresh blood and organs of snakes butchered for you on the spot – an experience providing a practical lesson in oriental philosophy and an initiation into the fundamental paradox of life within death. However, it may be a place best avoided by the faint-hearted. Instead try some typical Burmese herbal shampoo. Produced from a decoction of the bark of a shrub known as the *tagaw*, mixed with black acacia pods, it is sold in small plastic sachets and gives the hair a softness and shine. Cheroots are also available. These are made from tobacco, herbs, and roots and wrapped in maize leaves, to which an ashtray made from coconut is sometimes attached. Or try the coconut itself, served in the tradi-

If you visit the fish market on the Hlaing river in the early morning, you will see the boats come in. Once the catch is unloaded, the crews freshen up and have something to eat.

tional way: a blow of the machete slices the nut in two, like a wooden egg, transforming it into a gourd dripping with a delicious almond-flavoured milk. Some coconut vendors will leave you to divide the two halves by pressing with the palms of your hands while they make intimate predictions about your romantic future based on the sound of the cracking coconut.

The Burmese are quick to size up their clients and are never short of ideas to entertain the visitor. Prudence is recommended in this labyrinth of earthly delights, and it is important to remember that 'the light that breathes life into the shining flame of desire' inevitably ends in a flickering ember, and that a sudden flash of lightning can often lead to greater darkness. 'Do not allow the hours to pass by in shadow,' says the sage; 'discover the reality hidden behind appearance. Awaken yourself to the truth that liberates all forms of existence from the illusions, passions, and pain inherent therein.'

The principles of Buddhist belief were elaborated in the sixth century BC by the Buddha, also known as Siddhartha Gautama or Shakyamuni, the sage of the Shakya. Buddhism is derived from

Hinduism and seeks to free the individual from the eternal cycle of rebirth or samsara, which is determined in accordance with that person's good and bad deeds or karma. In Burma the Buddhist tradition relates to the 'Way of the Elders', the doctrine that is closest to the teachings of the Buddha and is known as Theravada or Hinayana Buddhism, or the 'Lesser Vehicle'. The adjective 'lesser' in no way implies that this doctrine is inferior to the 'Greater Vehicle' or Mahayana Buddhism, which prevails in Tibet, Nepal, Mongolia, Japan, China, and Vietnam. The characteristic of Lesser Vehicle Buddhism is an individual quest based on ascesis. In this system of belief nirvana is achieved through personal endeavour, the monastic life being the quintessential expression of this. The ideal sought is saintliness; this requires perfect understanding achieved through liberating oneself from the yoke of passion and impurity. Theravada Buddhism is in fact more a philosophy than a religion; the follower may practise whatever religion they choose while simultaneously following the teachings of the Buddha. The 'Four Noble Truths' of Buddhism will nevertheless inform the life of all followers:

Following pages:
Bamboo is still an important part of everyday life in Burma. The canes are tied together in rafts 10 metres [30 ft] long and floated downriver. At the day's end they are tied up at the river bank. They continue their journey downstream the next day.

1. Life is suffering.

2. The origin of suffering is desire.

3. Suffering can be ended by overcoming desire.

4. There is a path that leads to the suppression of suffering.

The path to deliverance is known in Theravada Buddhism as the Noble Eightfold Path. It consists of following eight principles: right views, right intentions, right speech, right action, right livelihood, right effort, right-mindedness, and right contemplation.

Each of these pathways has its rules, courses charted for the mind, which set out the methods to be followed. The first of these is strict abstention from all bad deeds, commencing with murder, theft, lust, untruthfulness, and the consumption of alcohol.

Other methods involve the use of psychological exercises such as meditation, to be performed several times a day. By focusing one's thoughts on certain ideas or images and concentrating on these, it is possible gradually to transform the mind; to apprehend the truth of the different articles of the doctrine; to rid oneself of illusions, of expressed ideas, and empty reasoning; to develop positive virtues;

The Pazundaung Creek river port on the outskirts of Rangoon is crowded with boats of all sizes. Huge teak-built junks transport timber from the forests of Burma to Singapore.

Because Burma is largely Buddhist, there are a large number of pagodas. The most sacred of these is the Shwedagon, which overlooks the capital from the 55-metre-high [180 ft] hill on which it stands. Ordination of monks and novices takes place frequently at the pagoda.

Opposite:
The Sule Pagoda in the heart of Rangoon offers weary believers an oasis of peace amid the bustle of the city.

to do away with the bad habits associated with the emotions; and finally to experience perfect tranquillity. The aim of all such exercises is to ensure that when one is reborn it is in improved circumstances. Buddhists seek to unburden their karma in order to reduce the number of their future reincarnations.

Nearly 85 per cent of the population of Burma is of the Buddhist faith, and the Shwedagon Pagoda in Rangoon is the country's most venerated shrine. It is said to contain eight of the Buddha's hairs, and its origins are clouded in myth. On a more realistic note, the British claimed that there was more gold on the Shwedagon than in the coffers of the Bank of England. The Shwedagon Pagoda is certainly one of the finest gold monuments in the Orient. Encrusted with 5,448 diamonds, 2,317 rubies, sapphires and topazes, and topped by an enormous, glistening emerald at a height of 100 metres

[over 300 feet], it stands perched above the city as if looking out over the abyss.

Though some may see the gold and precious stones as a display of wealth, for others they are a tribute expressed through the marriage between the sun and the stars lying within the earth. The Shwedagon is, above all, a source of spiritual inspiration to the people of Burma. Their veneration is resolute, faithful, and intense. Earthquakes and fires have failed to shake their determination to perpetuate its splendour. Whenever damage has occurred, the generosity of the faithful has enabled the pagoda to be restored and even enriched. It is a masterpiece of absolute mystery illuminating time.

The Shwedagon is the most revered pagoda in Burma and a place of pilgrimage for all Burmese monks, who come here to meditate and pray in the many pavilions surrounding the central stupa.
Preceding pages:
The stupa of the Shwedagon Pagoda has a circumference of 240 metres [785 ft]. The octagonal base is surrounded by sixty-four small golden pagodas.

*W*ood and stone sculpture blend harmoniously; the gold of the woodcarving
provides a warm contrast to the pastel tones of the capitals.

• Sacred architecture •

Burma is a country rich in teak, and its monastery buildings were originally constructed of wood.
The Burmese were highly accomplished carpenters, but unfortunately no trace of the early temples
remains.

The first monarch to leave his mark on the design of the stupa was King Anawratha. Around 1060,
to commemorate his conversion to Buddhism and affirm his political authority, the king ordered
the construction of the Shwesandaw Pagoda. The architectural design of the pagoda is on a
grandiose scale: there are five square terraces reached by axial stairways, two octagonal plinths,
and an impressive bell topped by golden parasols. The Shwezigon Pagoda, built around 1086, is more
artistic in style. The walls of the terraces are decorated with reliefs in glazed sandstone dominated
by an imposing golden bell.

*I*n pavilions, on altars, and in
prayer rooms there are countless
statues of the Buddha in all the
traditional poses, his face
illuminated by a smile of serenity.

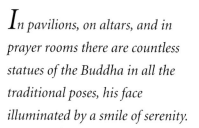

Bamboo is used to make furniture, among other things. After cutting, it is stacked in bundles to dry.
Opposite:
In the Burmese countryside women never go outdoors without applying 'thanaka' powder to their cheeks as they believe it protects them from both the sun and mosquitoes.

According to legend, Pegu – or Bago as it is also known – was originally a tiny island in the Gulf of Martaban, so small that a wild goose wishing to land there had to do so on the back of a gander. Two Mon princes from Thaton, witnessing the unusual encounter between the two birds, considered this to be a good omen and decided to found a city on the spot. Thus Pegu was first called Mamsawaddy or Hanthawady – the 'kingdom of the goose'.

From 1287 to 1599 Hanthawady was the centre of the Mon kingdom, and sixteenth-century European travellers brought back news of 'the existence of a flourishing town called Pegu, situated in Lower Myanmar'. In 1394 a daughter was born to King Razadorit in this mysterious city. She married King Ava, and at the age of about 30, against her husband's advice, the young queen decided to go into retreat in the company of two monks, who initiated her into the study of Buddhist scripture. The story of their sudden flight forms part of the repertoire of popular Burmese theatre. The two monks transform themselves into magicians, who confuse their pursuers by daily changing the colour of their boat.

By the time Queen Shinsawbu finally came to the throne, she was already 59, an age at which it was necessary for her to name her successor. In gratitude the queen decided to designate one of the monks who had been her mentors and escorts, but decreed that her choice would be determined by means of a competition, with the victor inheriting both the throne and the title of supreme king. Legend has it that Dhammazedi overcame his adversary by means of a magic formula which was to bring prosperity to the 'goose kingdom'.

In this, as in so many other stories of love and power, it is impossible to ascertain the true reality of what happened. It is through fiction alone and the subtleties of language that we are able to comprehend the abstract – through allegory and a sense of beauty derived always from an extremely shrewd combination of strategy (thought), desire (urge), and a profound sense of spirituality (the way to salvation).

Your Burmese guide will often finish this tale by telling you that Dhammazedi, who ruled for twenty years, transformed Pegu into the centre of Theravada Buddhism in South-East Asia and established relations with Europe. He may also tell you that this last monarch of the Mon people was a man of great charisma.

This last word is the key to the *res publica* whose interplay with the *res poetica* opens an anthology of *Pensées* to the visitor. These *Pensées*, like those of Pascal, the celebrated seventeenth-century French philosopher, are a fundamental revelation of the Absolute. The visitor is an incarnation of the time–space continuum, balancing on the frail cusp between fallen matter and glimpses of nirvana. Therefore be cautious when approaching the recumbent figure of the Swethalyaung. This Buddha is 55 metres [over 180 ft] in length and 16 metres [53 ft] tall. The statue's 'resurrection' is also an extraordinary tale involving this impalpable gravitation of spirituality, known in Burma as the light of time.

Created at the end of the tenth century, this great reclining Buddha was commissioned by the Mon king Migadhipa, who wished to leave behind a monumental sign of his conversion to Buddhism. It

*R*ice is still winnowed by hand in the traditional way.

was restored by Dhammazedi but later fell into decay. With the passage of time a protective layer of leaves and soil covered the statue until it was rediscovered by British engineers excavating material for railway embankment work. Did fate play a hand? We cannot tell, but we do know that the Buddhists had considerable difficulty in saving the statue from the British explosives experts. Today it looks down on us with that enigmatic smile that is the expression of the indefinable feeling experienced by the Enlightened One as he leaves his earthly prison and enters the path of holiness.

Pegu, like the celebrated communicating vessels of the deities, is a place where the natural and the supernatural come together. Visit the Mahazedi, built in 1560 by King Bayinnaung to enshrine a tooth of the Buddha. Fate dictated that it was at precisely this period that the Goan Portuguese, having attacked Ceylon, should return with considerable booty, including a golden tooth encrusted with precious stones. When King Bayinnaung heard this news, he offered a colossal sum for this relic, which was claimed to be the 'tooth of Kandy', the most sacred of all Buddhist relics.

*B*urma is primarily an agricultural country. Crops such as rice, sugar cane, and tobacco vary in importance according to the region.
Following pages:
Aquatic plants are grown in the canals and rivers of Burma; they can only be harvested by boat.

The city of Pegu has a number of interesting shrines, including the Kyaikpun Pagoda with its four seated Buddhas. The city also boasts Burma's finest statue of the Buddha reclining – the Shwethalyaung Buddha. This figure is 55 metres long and 16 metres high [180 ft long and 53 ft high], and represents Gautama Buddha about to enter nirvana, his face illuminated by a serene smile. It was restored in 1948.

Enticed by the sum, the vice-king of Goa was on the point of concluding the deal when fear of the Inquisition caused him to have this object of pagan veneration publicly destroyed. Some time later it was reported that the relic had appeared at the court of the king of Colombo. King Bayinnaung therefore decided to ask for the hand of the king's daughter in marriage, hoping to obtain the famous tooth as part of the dowry she would bring. However, their union had no sooner been made official than an emissary from Ceylon was sent to warn him that the 'tooth of Kandy' had never left their island. Nevertheless, the king still decided to have the tooth set into the Mahazedi.

Following the conquest of Pegu in 1539, the false relic – assuming it was indeed false – was taken to Toungoo, then to Sagaing near Mandalay, where it was enshrined in the Kaunghmudaw Pagoda near the city, together with an alms bowl believed to have been made by the Buddha himself. There it remains, ready and waiting for its next peregrination.

*E*very year between November and March numerous pilgrimages take place to the shrine
at the summit of Mount Kyaiktiyo amid an atmosphere of intense religious fervour.

• The Golden Rock •

The Kyaiktiyo or Golden Rock Pagoda is one of the most unusual shrines in Burma. A small stupa
7.3 metres [24 ft] high has been built on top of a large rock covered in gold leaf that balances
mysteriously on the edge of a cliff.

Legend has it that the rock is balanced by a strand of the Buddha's hair enshrined in the stupa. It
is said that the hair was given to King Tissa by a hermit who had received it directly from the Buddha
himself during a visit.

The king, who was endowed with magical powers, took from the sea-bed a rock resembling the
head of the hermit. He placed it in a boat which miraculously came to rest on the summit of Mount
Kyaiktiyo. This rock is still visible from a distance of some 300 metres [1,000 ft] and is known as
Kyauktanban or the 'stupa of the boat of stone'.

Four of the Buddha's teeth are enshrined in the Shwezayan Pagoda in Thaton. The building dates back to the fifth century BC.

The cities of Thaton and Pegu share similar histories. According to legend, two missionaries sent by Emperor Ashoka founded the city, and Thaton's Shwezayan Pagoda enshrines not one, but four of the Buddha's teeth.

Thaton is the capital of the Mon region. Situated on the Gulf of Martaban, it became the centre of Theravada Buddhism and, once this branch of the Buddhist faith was established, the birthplace of Buddhist art. In Burmese the word for pagoda is *paya*, which also means sacred, and is a term applied to geographical, spiritual, and even sociological entities. Most often it is used to refer to the architectural feature known as a stupa. Two types of *paya* or stupa exist: the *zedi (chedi)* and the *patho*. The first are bell-like rounded forms, whereas the latter are square or rectangular. The two structures have complementary religious functions. The *zedi* normally enshrines relics of the Buddha (bones, teeth, and hair) while the *patho* is a temple or shrine.

*Moulmein, with its 300,000
inhabitants, is the third largest city
in Burma and the capital of the Mon
state. A covered stairway leads to the
Kyaikthanlan Pagoda, which
overlooks the town and port, from
which rice and teak were once
exported.*

Under the British, between 1827 and 1852, Moulmein was the administrative seat of Burma. It was also famous for its shipyards, which provided ships for the opium trade supplying China from Bengal and Malwa in India. The East India Company too, which in 1833 had lost its trading monopoly, drew its main source of income from contraband. The sailing boats used by the opium dealers were built mainly from teak, and their speed and manoeuvrability made it easy for them to evade the Chinese coast-guards. Where these shipyards once stood, there are now sawmills and rice-processing factories, but the post-colonial atmosphere still pervades the city. Moulmein is the capital of the Mon state and, with 300,000 inhabitants, the third largest city in Burma.

Dawei Jetty Road runs from the Dawei ferry dock to the end of the corniche leading to the city's most important temples. The road itself is rich in history – a Chinese temple stands alongside a Baptist church, reflecting Moulmein's varied past. However, the most culturally interesting building must be the Mon museum.

The Mon people, once the dominant ethnic group in Burma, have

been gradually supplanted by the immigrating Burmans. The Mons speak an Austro-Asiatic language, and they may have entered Burma from China, descending the Mekong with the Khmer. Together they founded a kingdom whose name in Sanskrit (Swannabhumi) means 'the golden land'. The capital enjoyed great prosperity up to the twelfth century. It exerted a key social and political influence over the two economic centres of southern India and Ceylon. However, when King Anawratha took control of the city in the early eleventh century, he moved the capital to Bagan, which became the capital of the first Burmese Empire.

The Mon people, known for many years by the pejorative term of Talaing, are now only a small community of some 1.3 million people; the majority of the remaining members of the Mon–Khmer community live in Vietnam, Cambodia, and Thailand.

The great Shwezayan stupa is part of Mon heritage, but it has been altered to such an extent over the centuries that it is impossible to imagine how it originally appeared. Nevertheless, comparisons with other remnants of Mon culture make it possible to identify some

of its key architectural features. Monastery enclosures were generally marked by stone pillars, and the plinths and base of the stupas were sculpted or decorated with reliefwork either made of lime mortar or fashioned from clay and then baked. These reliefs depicted scenes from the life of the Buddha in accordance with canonical rules set out in Buddhist texts and embellished by legends inspired by local people or places.

The Mon museum of culture, though on a modest scale, contains steles bearing inscriptions and ancient items of carved wood used in monasteries for the education of young monks. The museum also holds a considerable amount of ceramic work, furniture, silver betel boxes, lacquerware, funeral urns, musical instruments, and wooden altars to the Buddha.

From the top of the Kyaikthanlan *paya* there is a view over islands covered in coconut palms. One of these, Kyun Gaungse or 'hair-wash island', now better known as Shampœ Island, takes its name from the fourteenth-century ritual ceremony that accompanied the washing of the royal hair with spring water from the island.

Only the sounds of the market and the call of the muezzin from the mosque disturb the provincial tranquillity of the Mon capital.

Off the Tenasserim coast lie the 840 islands that make up the Mergui archipelago. Although the area was inaccessible to foreigners for many years, tourism is now being developed here.

Following pages:

The Mergui archipelago has hundreds of kilometres of coastline and its inhabitants live mainly from the sea. For some years now Mergui pearl fishers have worked for Japanese companies. The region is also famous for a type of edible swallows' nest found here.

Mergui is the capital of Burma's Tanintharyi division and is situated on the coast near the mouth of the Tanintharyi river. It is a port at the end of the world, built on a strip of land projecting into the Andaman Sea. The town, known locally as Beik or Myeith, lies under a deep blue sky flecked with purple and white and, like some crouching animal, appears poised, exuberant yet indifferent, cut off from the rest of the world.

Visitors will find it difficult to gain access to much of the Tanintharyi region, and special authorisation is often needed to visit the Myeik or Mergui islands, which comprise one of the most beautiful archipelagos in South-East Asia. There are some 840 islands scattered along the coastline, and they still provide a haven for the Salon, also known as the 'sea gypsies'.

These are the descendants of the fearsome smugglers who once worked for middlemen operating from the hinterland. Back in the interior strange stories of their exploits are still recounted. At nightfall oil lamps are lit in the street stalls and an air of mystery pervades the archipelago. The proximity of the sea brings peace to the soul,

*T*housands of houses built on piles line each bank of the Tanintharyi river.

• The art of living •

The Burmese are a people strongly attached to the traditions which shape their lives. When a child is born, an astrologer is summoned. It is his job to determine the character traits of the child. The child is not named until seven days have passed, and the name given is determined by the child's character. Children start their schooling at 5 years old. A boy brought up in the Buddhist tradition carries out his *shin pyu* between the ages of 7 and 12, during which he wears the saffron robes of the Buddhist priests. He becomes 'a son of Buddha' and follows a series of rituals based on study, retreat, and a number of ceremonies. For a girl the rite of passage is marked only by ear-piercing, which is carried out shortly before puberty.

The Burmese tend to marry quite young. Marriage does not involve any particular religious or civil ceremony; all that is required is a formal registration before the authorities guaranteeing the division of property in case of divorce. In Burma women enjoy the same rights as men.

and the hollow-cheeked old men resemble silent idols, embodying the unspoken.

During the eighteenth century Mergui was an important port serving the Thai kingdom of Ayuthaya. Goods were loaded there, and passengers embarked to sail up the river Tanintharyi in small boats. Mergui then became an important trading centre and was occupied by the British after the first Anglo-Burmese war of 1826. On certain days, when the sky grows heavy and grey, the British elements of the town combine with the tropical to produce a strange blend: the river banks resemble the margins of the Thames – but depleted, shrivelled, eaten away by a vaporous sea.

Nowadays the archipelago's main sources of income are rubber, coconuts, and the sea. *Ngapi*, a highly prized fermented fish paste, is one local product, but the archipelago's principal gastronomic delicacy is the terns' nests collected by agile locals. The birds make their nests from saliva which hardens on contact with the air. The nests are usually cooked in a chicken stock, becoming soft and separating into a kind of noodle, and are said to possess aphrodisiac properties.

To collect the nests the locals use a structure made from lianas and bamboo and, with great skill and daring, hoist themselves up under the roofs of the huge limestone caves, which are often inaccessible at high tide. In the local cafés in the evening the exploits of these new athletes are increasingly replacing old pirates' tales – though there are some who will tell you that the latter have not altogether disappeared.

During the nineteenth century the sea gypsies operated in close collaboration with other organisations and between them control-led the whole of the China Sea and the Indian Ocean from the Sunda islands, via Malaysia to the Bay of Along. They were excel-lent sailors and possessed *prahu* (vessels for attack), *penjajap*, and *lanong* – long, narrow, twin-masted, deckless boats with quadran-gular sails and twenty or thirty oarsmen. The boats were armed with two small bronze culverins in the bows and escorted by the lighter and faster *kapap* used for reconnaissance and for river ascent. They hunted in packs of six or eight, sometimes more, and only rarely did their prey escape. In the broad silk sash around their

The 840 islands that make up the archipelago are home to the 'sea gypsies' who, until recently, had a reputation as ferocious pirates.

Sheltering in a small cove beneath a white pagoda lies the village of Chao Pya. Hundreds of fishermen live here in houses built on piles, with roofs made of palm leaves.

waist these men carried the notorious *kris*, the fearsome, magical knife whose blade was scalloped like a flame. To this these pirates would often add a richly carved and ornamented sabre, a round shield, sometimes a spear used as a javelin, and possibly a pistol as a prestige item. Their bodies were covered in tattoos which they believed won them the favour of the *nat* and made them invulnerable. Boardings were executed with extraordinary agility. In only a few minutes the crew of the boarded vessel knew that any resistance would be futile. The plundering of the prey took place with remarkable dexterity and speed. The cargo was sorted into those items that could be sold off cheaply and other more valuable booty. All this was often carried out without blood being shed or unnecessary violence, and the pirates remained answerable to their chiefs on this account.

Magnificent coconut groves and deserted beaches can be found on the sparsely populated island of Kalar.

Piracy, which had originally been on a small scale, gradually became more organised. Local potentates secretly funded these expeditions, financing them with loans for armaments, rigging, and so on. Huge campaigns were mounted, particularly with the arrival of western-ers. Items being sent from Europe to the warehouses of eastern ports, and especially those in Mergui, became much sought after. Orders were even placed to obtain western beauties, and it is claimed that some of those of mixed race are the result of what is euphemistically referred to as 'sentimental' piracy.

Nowadays, at that time of day when a breath of air seems like the draft from a giant fan, when the songs of the earth travel down to the sea, there is a magical moment when it seems that everything blends, intermingles, and interpenetrates. 'In the centre of the sea lies Mieck' – these are the words of a song which tells the story of a queen wandering lost in the labyrinth of shadows who is saved by the harps that the sea gypsies play at night.

Now the old stories are becoming a thing of the past and their place is being taken by new characters who symbolise modern life and the

world of business. One such is U Nya Aye, a Burmese of Chinese extraction, who has become one of Myeik's wealthiest citizens. It is said that the swallows nest in his living room and that harvesting nests has given him an income of over 400,000 kyats a year. Swallows' nests have become so highly sought after that they are known as the archipelago's 'white gold', fetching as much as 2,000 dollars a kilo.

When one realises that the city of Hong Kong alone imports 25 million dollars' worth of nests, it is obvious that U Nya Aye need have no concern about his future livelihood, and the same is true of all those other nest collectors living like nomads on small boats and dropping anchor in the bays of the archipelago to shelter from the storms and collect their precious booty. Many of these people – who are also known as the Moken – make a living from the sea in other traditional ways handed down over the generations. Pearl fishing is one example. The Moken diver attaches stone weights around his waist, enabling him to reach a depth of 60 metres [nearly 200 ft] while continuing to breathe through a long tube, the tip of

which remains above the surface of the water. Nowadays these fishermen work mainly for Japanese companies.

According to recent studies, Mergui has a bright future in tourism with its crystal-clear waters, ivory beaches, and unspoilt hinterland. And when night falls an ineffable presence seems to purify the buildings, which become no more than walls encircled by stars.

A common sight in the shallow waters between the islands is the wooden posts in the mud where local fishermen have set up hoop nets.
Following pages:
The fishermen's huts are simple and basic.

Opposite:
On a beach near Bassein stands a
rocky outcrop venerated by the
locals. A small pagoda has been
erected on the top to denote its
sacred character.

Bassein was originally known as Pathein, a name derived from *pathi*, which in Burmese means Muslim. This was because for centuries it was the largest port on the Irrawaddy delta and an important trading post for Indian and Arab merchants. It was rechristened Bassein when the British moved in during the nineteenth century.

Today the town is the centre of a rice-growing area producing the best rice in Myanmar, the *pawsanmwe htamin* or aromatic rice. Bassein is also famous for its hand-painted parasols, which give the town a nostalgic air. Against the backdrop of the river the silhouettes of passers-by seem like delicate insects ready to take to their wings in the twilight.

The Irrawaddy river provides a means of transport southwards for teak and bamboo.
Preceding pages:
In this branch of the Irrawaddy delta many small boats provide a means of crossing the river.

Prome or Pyi is situated on a bend in the Irrawaddy river. It was once a trading post used by Indian and Sinhalese merchants. In those days the town was the port of the ancient Pyu capital Thackhittya, 8 km [5 miles] north-east of Prome. Since 1907 the most extensive excavation work in Myanmar has taken place at this site. During the course of the sixth and seventh centuries a new kind of art developed in Prome. It combined the influences of the Indian and Mon peoples with the constructional genius of the Pyu. Its principal characteristics lie in the depiction of movement and use of colour, as demonstrated in the many examples of bronze sculpture and motifs. Some of the royal reliquaries also display the refined engraving techniques used on both stone and semi-precious stones such as dolomite, quartz, and rock crystal. They form part of a quite remarkable tradition in Burmese art.

The architectural style of Pagan originated in the religious buildings of Prome. The city in fact became a cultural crossroads of seminal influence and is a place of profound significance to the cultural identity of the Burmese people.

The Shwesandaw Pagoda is the city's principal attraction and is also one of Burma's main centres of Buddhist pilgrimage. The pagoda is believed to enshrine some of the Buddha's hair, hence the name Shwesandaw, which means 'relic of the golden hair'.

Naturally the significance of this relic goes far beyond its mere material presence. It is the corporeal expression of a mystery whose presence can at times be sensed in the silence of the evening. Discovering the element of truth within a symbol is a challenge that requires profound meditation, a challenge which turns its back on emotional distraction or fleeting inspiration. It is an encounter with a deep and powerful force, such as is reflected in the chanting of the monks.

The Shwesandaw Pagoda is an imposing structure. The *zedi* here is more than 1 metre [3 ft] taller than the main *zedi* at the Shwedagon and, like the Shwezigan Pagoda in Bagan, is of classical construction. Built on the top of a hill, it overlooks an enormous statue of the Buddha which emerges like an apparition above the treetops to the east, fixing you with its eyes. Some Buddhist disciples believe

that the statue possesses an almost vibratory energy, a mysterious revitalising power emanating from its gaze and clarifying the message concealed behind external appearance: that awareness of exile from the world is the precondition of access to the heart of the Buddha's truth.

Eight kilometres [5 miles] to the south-west of Prome lie the ruins of Sri Ksetra, the ancient capital of the Pyu kingdom. The Pyu had descended from the foothills of Tibet and settled in the valley of the Upper Irrawaddy. They were a farming people and are believed to have migrated there around the fourth century BC. However, of the ruins that lie scattered within the vast circular area some 13 km [9 miles] round, the oldest date back to the fifth and sixth centuries. Coming across the stone shells scattered among the vegetation, one becomes even more aware of the spiritual quality emanating from such sites. Among these lost temples, the wreckages of time, a mysterious aroma seems to hang in the air, reminiscent of some secret alchemy of transmutation. They stand now exposed in all their purity to the brilliance of the sun.

Life revolves around the river and the riverbank; small red plums are spread out on straw mats to dry in the sun.

*P*rome is a fertile agricultural
region producing a variety of crops.
The principal means of transport for
local produce, such as turnips and
ground nuts, is the ox cart.

The site at Sri Ksetra is the ancient capital of Pyu civilisation. Pagodas of varying forms still remain: the Payagyi and the Payama are conical; the Bawbawgi and the Bebe are cylindrical. For almost a century the site at Sri Ksetra has attracted more archaeologists than any other in Burma.

The oldest temple is the Bawbawgi, which dates from the sixth century. It is 46 metres [150 ft] high and stands on five superposed terraces. The stupas, which are either solid or contain a reliquary chamber, are slightly conical in form and borrow from the Indian style, but all are built on multiple terraces. Some have been raised on a high, square base decorated with ornamental terracotta plaques. The first shrines stand nearby.

The Bebe temple is a simple cubic plinth open to the east and topped by a stupa of three blocks of diminishing proportions. The external walls are decorated with pilasters, and within is a vaulted room on the far wall of which is a representation of the Buddha with a disciple on either side of him.

This is not a place for the hurried tourist. It is a sacred place where solitary acts of worship to his immanent majesty may be performed. In this temple timelessness, the residence and resonance of being, is crystallised. The universe, though infinitely close, requires much time in the approach.

Next to the site of the ancient palace there is a small museum dis-

playing a collection of objects discovered by archaeologists. These include votive tablets, royal funeral urns, bas-reliefs, statues of the Buddha and Hindu deities, and silver coins struck in this kingdom about which we know so little.

A Chinese chronicle from the Tang dynasty (618–905) includes this description of life in the Pyu kingdom: 'When the king of the Pyu people goes out, he does so on a palanquin and reclines on a golden mat. When covering long distances he sits astride an elephant. Several hundred women keep watch over him ... The Pyus are Buddhists and have some hundred monasteries built in glazed brick decorated in gold and silver.' We know that up to the ninth century the city of Sri Ksetra enjoyed great prosperity, before falling victim to tribal warfare. Two centuries later it fell prey to Anawratha, who had the walls razed to the ground after removing the relics from its temples to adorn those of his capital, Pagan.

*I*n the centre of the city, overlooking
the valley of the Irrawaddy, stands
the Shwesandaw Pagoda with its
golden stupas under the watchful
guard of the Chinthé lion. Many
statues of the Buddha – large, small,
and multi-faced – lie concealed
along the paths of the surrounding
countryside.

Every morning, shortly after sunrise, monks and novices set out from their temples with their alms bowls in their hands to collect offerings of food made by the faithful. In the entrance gallery to the Shwesandaw Pagoda there are shops with religious souvenirs on sale to pilgrims and the faithful.

Toungoo was once the centre of one of Burma's most flourishing kingdoms, but today almost nothing remains of its glorious fifteenth- and sixteenth-century past. The town's commerce still relies principally on the timber harvested from the mountain ranges surrounding it to the west and east. In fact almost half of Burma is covered by unexploited primary forests, but only 15 per cent of these contains teak or hardwoods. Many wild animals live in these vast expanses of virgin forest. Among those hunted are the tiger, leopard, wild buffalo, the red deer, wild boar, the Himalayan black bear, and the Malayan bear. Although it is the world's smallest bear, the Malayan has a reputation for being particularly fierce. Today Toungoo is known in Burma for the cultivation of the areca palm, the fruit of which is used to make betel. The flowers of the betel plant – a variety of climbing

pepper – are blended with cloves, aniseed, tobacco leaves, licorice, and areca nuts to produce this chewable, astringent substance widely used by the people of South-East Asia.

However, it is the crumbling forms and faded colours of the town's historical monuments that give the place its mysterious and individual character. Their decaying presence is a constant reminder of mortality. In Toungoo this quality is embodied most clearly in the Shwesandaw Pagoda. The temple was constructed at the end of the sixteenth century on the site of a stupa in which sacred hairs of the Buddha were enshrined. To the west of the central monument stands a building housing a large seated Buddha made of bronze. Nearby is another statue of the Buddha, this time reclining inside a pavilion. There is also a *nat* shrine and a series of representations creating a space where a great variety of signs act as markers leading to the spiritual Idea. The purpose is to demonstrate that we exist in a space that is the product of both mental positioning and cosmic choreography. Here time becomes an ocean and, like so many mooring lines, it is our position that holds us fast amid the

Preceding pages:
Chilli peppers are grown in abundance throughout the Toungoo and Meiktila region. At harvest time the pavements of the towns and villages are transformed into a sea of red.
The province also produces a large amount of sugar cane, which is transported by lorry to nearby processing plants.

In this agricultural region ox and buffalo carts are still the principal means of transport.

tempests of passion and desire. Through this symbolism death is dissolved in the omnipresence of nature, and the Buddha alone offers the possibility of consummation.

Myasigon houses an enormous seated Buddha with a bronze and silver face, which invites another form of meditation that will lead us to a state of extreme lucidity presaging the nothingness which threatens all our destinies. The traveller who has reached this stage of the journey will now enter the pathway that leads to true glory. Paintings depicting the kings of Toungoo and vaults covered in glass mosaic serve both as historical reminders and as initiatory links that help resolve the enigma of the path of silence that equips the follower with the weapons they need in their spiritual battle.

The Burmese pantheon is a welcoming one. What matters is that one should enter upon the Eightfold Path leading to this inexhaustible reserve of truth that those enamoured of the absolute find in the spiritual law of Theravada Buddhism, and where for millions of the faithful the mask-like features of the representation are transfigured into the face of the Buddha.

In Toungoo the remnants of the past become a heady force, and wordplay challenges the spirit already exposed to the deep-rooted symbolism of a boundless poesy. This continual participation involves nature in a secret alchemy where the bouquet of colours, the power of odours, and the tactile sensations are so strong that one recognises intuitively that the existence of each element depends as much on the presence of the others as on itself.

The splendours of the ancient kingdom of Toungoo are now reduced to a few ruined earthworks and a moat to the west of the town. Close by, the 'royal lake', with its scattering of small pavilion-covered islands, seems like a pictorial scheme of signs reconciling the obscure pathways of dreams with the lucidity of metaphysical enlightenment. Towards the western side of the lake stands the Kawmudaw Pagoda, the most ancient of the religious sites. Pilgrims who visit this place walk around the monument in an anticlockwise direction to absorb the radiated energy which, they believe, will enable them to resolve their problems.

Although rickshaws are normally reserved for passenger transport, they are sometimes used to carry light but bulky items.

In the Thargaya forest elephants are used to drag logs out from the undergrowth. Three thousand elephants are involved in hauling timber in Burma.

*S*omewhat unusually, country markets are held every five days. Although it may be easy to locate the site of the markets, it can be difficult to make visits coincide with market day.

Meiktila is an important and prosperous centre of trade with a strong tradition of craftwork. The Burmese remain firmly attached to their traditions and are famous for the quality of their art and craftwork. In the past the exquisite lacquerwork bowls produced in Burma were much sought after. These were usually made from horsehair woven on a frame of bamboo. Goldwork is still very much in evidence, a notable example being the gold leaf applied to the Buddhist pagodas and statues. The gold originates from deposits in the north of Burma. The nuggets are hammered flat until they are no thicker than a sheet of paper. Silverwork is less important now than it once was, but work in copper and brass is still as active as ever. Craftsmen create statues of the Buddha, gongs, bells for pagodas and monasteries, and also smaller bells for use with livestock. Burmese marble craftsmen are still

Unlike many other Asian peoples, the Burmese proudly continue to wear the traditional cotton 'longyi' tied around their waist. In the Meiktila region many villagers dye and weave cotton thread and produce the finest 'longyi' or sarong in Burma.

highly regarded, for their monumental masonry work in particular. Woodcarving remains an important activity.

The Burmese have earned a fine reputation for weaving and embroidery and still use traditional dyeing methods based on recipes handed down from generation to generation. Of course, for many people the name Myanmar is synonymous with jewels, and particularly precious stones. Many glittering red, green, and purple gemstones can be found, but the most prized stone is the ruby, of which Burma remains the world's largest producer.

The history of precious stones in Burma goes back many years. Before the British gained power, it was nurtured for centuries under the Burmese kings. Today the mines have been nationalised, but there is still a considerable amount of 'unofficial' trading in the markets of Burma, with some markets under the control of the outlying regions, which are the major producers of gemstones. These areas are also the strongholds of ethnic minorities demanding political autonomy – their armed rebellions have been financed from the proceeds of smuggling precious stones.

*Mount Popa is considered to be home to the most powerful 'nat' spirits in Myanmar
and is therefore a very important cultural centre.
Halfway up the hillside a shrine contains the statues of the thirty-seven official 'nat' of Myanmar.
Monasteries cover the rocky escarpment.*

• Mount Popa •

In Sanskrit the word *popa* means 'flower', and the countryside surrounding Burma's Mount Olympus is like an enchanted garden. From the summit of the rock the view is exceptional.

In former times many alchemists and occultists lived in the surrounding area. Mount Popa is 1,520 metres [5,000 ft] high and dominates the plain on which it stands. Geologically speaking, it is a volcano, but has been extinct for 250,000 years. The fertile ash it deposited and its rain-producing microclimate have produced a miracle of nature. Years ago elephants, rhinoceroses, and tigers roamed the surrounding forests. Twice a year, during the two great festivals held in honour of the *nat*, Mount Popa becomes the most popular venue in Burma. These festivals take place during the Nayan full moon (May to June) and the Nadaw full moon (November to December). The climb to the top of the mountain is steep and takes about twenty minutes. Red or black should not be worn while making the ascent; swearing and speaking ill of others are also frowned upon.

The ruins at Pagan extend over some 25 sq km [9 sq miles] along the bank of the Irrawaddy river. The site contains many ochre-coloured temples and pagodas.
Most of these monuments are brick-built, sometimes with sandstone elements.
To visit the whole site takes at least three days as the pagodas are spread out across the arid plain.

In Pagan (or Bagan) Theravada Buddhism finds its finest expression. Of the 5,000 pagodas which occupied the site during the thirteenth and fifteenth centuries, 2,219 remain to enthral visitors. The history of Pagan is directly associated with a prophecy made by the Buddha. Having attained the state of enlightenment, the Buddha undertook a long journey, in the course of which he passed through Pagan. The 'Chronicle of the Crystal Palace' recounts how, while in Pagan, a white heron, a black crow, a spirit, and a toad crossed the Buddha's path, and according to Buddhist sources, 'Siddhartha made the following prophecy: 651 years after my parinirvana* a great kingdom will arise in this place. The presence of the white heron and the black crow in the top of the butea tree means that most of the people living there will be charitable and virtuous. Some of course will be bad people. The presence of the spirit means that not all those living in this kingdom will be farmers; some will live from commerce, and their words will not always be truthful. And the little toad squatting at the foot of the tree is a sign that people will be happy.'

* Parinirvana means 'total extinction'. It is a synonym for nirvana, referring to the moment that precedes, coincides with, or follows the death of a Buddha.

Thamuddarit, a Pyi king, is believed to have founded the town early in the second century, but it was not until the reign of Anawratha that Pagan began a period of remarkable expansion. Anawratha was a great monarch who exercised a powerful unifying force over Burma. Having conquered Thaton in Lower Burma, he determined to raise Pagan to the rank of political and spiritual capital of his empire. The king embarked on an ambitious building programme, both to celebrate his conversion to Buddhism and to give the region every necessary protection to ensure himself a successful reincarnation. Buddhist monuments covered the plain of Pagan, the most outstanding of these being the Shwesandaw Pagoda, which is also known as the Temple of Ganesh after the Hindu god of wisdom. This policy of major works continued during the reign of Kyanzittha (1108–1112), whose amorous and warlike exploits form part of the annals of Burmese poetry. It was Kyanzittha who built the Ananda Pagoda, an architectural masterpiece whose majestic white form dominates the plain. Although badly damaged by an earthquake in 1975, it has now been completely restored. The central block is 53 metres [174 ft] wide and is raised on terraces to a height of 51 metres [168 ft].

In his famous chronicle of 1298 Marco Polo wrote of Pagan: 'The towers are built of fine stone, some of which have then been covered with a layer of gold as thick as a finger. Thus it seems that the tower is made entirely of gold. The same is true of the towers covered in silver. According to his pleasure the king has chosen to erect these towers to commemorate the splendour of his reign and for the peace of his soul. The result is there for all to see. The towers have made this one of the most beautiful sites in the world, superb and precious with extreme attention to detail in the finishing. Bathed in sunlight, they sparkle brightly in the light, and their brilliance can be seen from a great distance.'

Today Pagan stands as a magnificent reliquary of Buddhist Awakening and holiness.

Only a few buildings, such as the Ananda Monastery, contain murals depicting scenes from the life of the Buddha.
Nearby, in a niche in the Sarabha Gate, the guardian spirit of the former Burmese capital keeps watch over this tranquil site.

During the last few years Mandalay, the capital of the north, has become an important commercial centre. The Zegyo market is awash with food and manufactured goods produced in China.

The history of Mandalay, like that of Pagan, is associated with a prophecy made by the Buddha. According to tradition, during a visit to the region with his loyal servant Ananda, Gautama Buddha declared that a 'Buddhist city' would be built at the foot of a hill 2,400 years later. King Mindon decided to make this prophecy a reality and commissioned a group of religious buildings to be erected in the hope that these temples would atone for the injustices perpetrated during his reign. In 1857 the 'golden city' was transferred from Amarupa to Mandalay, and in 1861 the new king moved into the city with the 100,000 inhabitants of his former capital. However, the course of history was to take an abrupt turn. In November 1895 King Thibaw, faced with advancing British troops, signed the surrender of the city, and General Prendergast rechristened the Burmese king's palace Fort Dufferin.

In March 1945 the fortress, which was being held by the Japanese, was shelled by the British air force and King Mindon's former palace was destroyed. The only parts to survive were the ramparts, the moats and foundations of the palace, and King Mindon's mauso-

The most famous building in Sagaing, the Kaunghmudaw Dome, was constructed in 1636 to enshrine a relic of the Buddha. Built in the Sinhalese style, according to legend the temple represents the perfectly formed breast of the wife of King Thalun.

leum. Today the Burmese army occupies the 'Mandalay Fort', but the government has started reconstruction work with the aim of turning the site into one of the area's main tourist attractions.

To visit Mandalay, start by climbing the hill that overlooks the city – there are 1,729 steps to climb or there is an optional lift or minibus. This stairway is like the first part of an initiation leading the visitor into the first temple, known as 'the Peshawar relics'; the relics referred to are three of the Buddha's bones believed to have been taken from his funeral pyre. To comprehend the relic cult, it is important to understand that for the believer these remains are the expression of a great conceptual vessel and that the human relics act as a compass indicating the path to salvation. Each follower must go beyond the multifariousness of their existence and seek to revive the essence leading to the threshold of that enigmatic space which is nirvana. The relics also symbolise the end of a particular life; the antechamber to this purer space is metaphysical in form and is akin to the idea of baptism, through which death in this world makes it possible to be reborn in a holier place.

The method of salvation discovered and taught by the Buddha is known as 'supramundane' (lokottara) because those who practise it are led forever out of the land of the dead and of rebirth, freed from the successive incarnations which are by their very nature painful – which is why nirvana (extinction) is also known as 'the gate to immortality'. It leads to a place 'beyond this world', where one enters a state that is inconceivable and ineffable, bearing no relation to our universe.

Near the top of the hill a massive golden Buddha stands guard. His extended hand signifies that his prophecy has been fulfilled and that his glorious presence bears witness to the state of disintegration in which we exist. And divided souls that we are, we do indeed search in desperation for our spiritual law.

The ogress Sanda Moke Khit stands guard at the foot of the Buddha. Having discovered his teachings, she decided to devote the rest of her life to the dharma, the essential principle of the cosmos derived from the natural order of all that exists. She cut off her breasts in honour of her conversion to the Buddhist way of life.

The Sandamuni Pagoda contains 1,774 stone tablets on which are engraved the Buddhist Tipitaka scriptures.
Following pages:
The village of Mingun can only be reached by boat. As well as its whitewashed pagodas the site also boasts the world's largest bell.

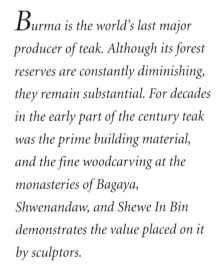

Burma is the world's last major producer of teak. Although its forest reserves are constantly diminishing, they remain substantial. For decades in the early part of the century teak was the prime building material, and the fine woodcarving at the monasteries of Bagaya, Shwenandaw, and Shewe In Bin demonstrates the value placed on it by sculptors.

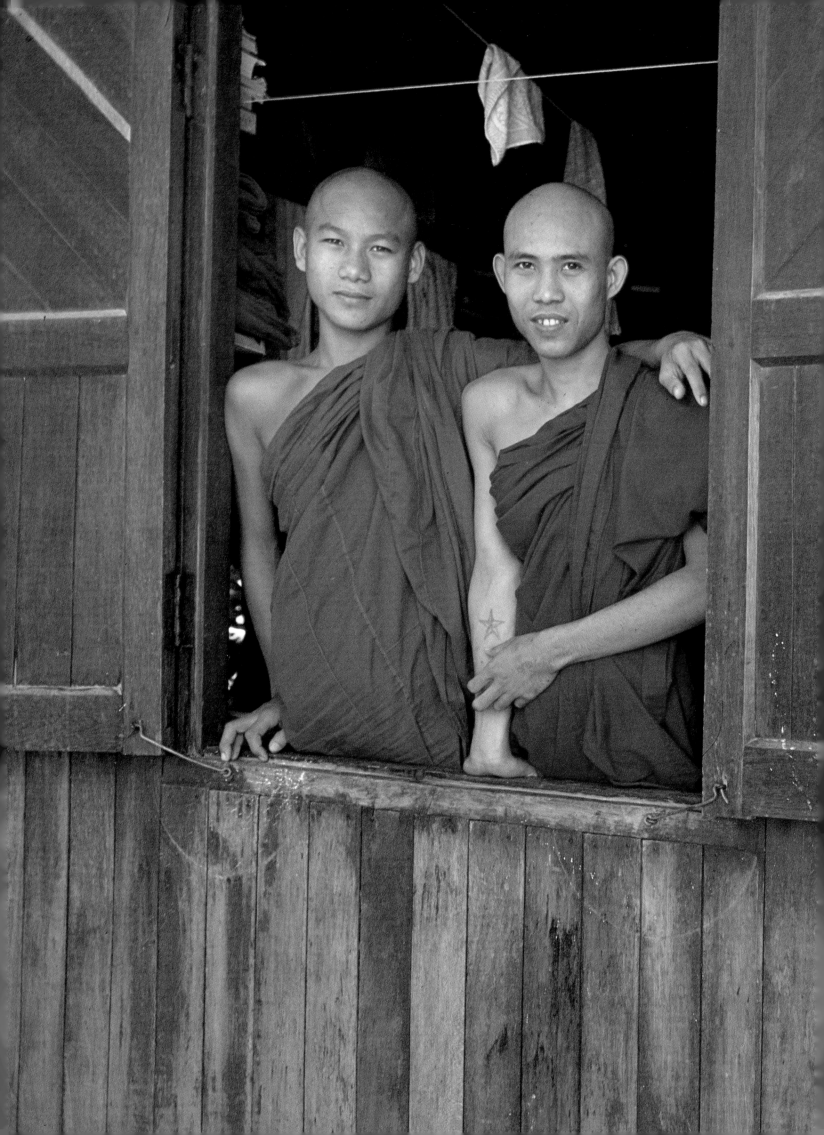

In the villages in the highlands to the north of Mandalay the main activity is growing flowers for the city's markets.

As is so often the case in Burma, the riverbank is a hive of activity. Here on the Irrawaddy, teak that has been floated downriver is removed from the water's edge by buffalo. Craftsmen work with bamboo that has also been carried down from the highlands by river.

From the point of view of Buddhism, the history of Burma is like a maze of pathways complicated by a fantastical game of mirrors. One needs to know how to outwit both danger and seduction in order to re-establish judgement and authority over worldly things. A double focus is needed that will make it possible to go beyond mere fabrication and attain this other perception of the world. False truths and true falsehoods are the dual aspects of a reality consumed in the spiritual intensity concealed within the inner temple, where the flame of enigma lights the way for true travellers on the pathway of truth.

The most sacred shrine in Mandalay, the Mahamuni, is also associated with another legend belonging to the time of the Buddha's sojourn in this region. It is said that the Buddha 'left behind an image of himself'. Historians still disagree on the exact date when this statue was created, but legend has it that it was Thagyamin, the king of the *nat*, who created the Mahamuni statue.

The secret of the gods comes from the desire to create a mystery, whereas the strength of an enigma comes from its interrogative power. According to the Buddhist tradition, this power is revealed on several levels which come together in the single word *kah*, meaning 'who?' Within *kah* the who is simply the echo of an enigma revealed, in response, in the smile of the Buddha.

A visit to the Tanshwe Pagoda, with its numerous limestone outcrops topped by stupas, can be an unusually active and entertaining experience for visitors.

The Kayah state is a mountainous region enclosed by the Shan state to the north and west, the Karen state to the west and south, and Thailand to the east. It is home to eight ethnic groups. The Kayah people are also known as the Karens or Red Karen because of their fondness for the colour red, and in particular for wearing red clothes. Their ceremonial rituals are very colourful, particularly the annual Kuhtobo festival held in May in honour of the rain spirits.

The Kayah state has a monsoon climate, with alternating dry and wet seasons. Its inhabitants live from agriculture, growing vegetables, millet, and rice by means of irrigation. After months without rainfall the Karens are impatient for the heavy, rain-laden clouds that will bring relief to their land. When they finally appear – vast, dark clouds that poets have likened to elephants in the air – and unleash their precious cargo in sudden torrential downpours, the people of Kayah embrace this rainfall with delight.

The parched, cracked earth soaks up the rain, a gift from the heavens, absorbing it greedily as Indra, the Hindu god of the

weather, becomes intoxicated on soma, the liquor of immortality. It is Indra who, with his glistening weapon of pure diamonds, bursts the heavy, black monsoon clouds appearing between May and October and releases the water that will render the land fertile.

The alternating seasons have led farmers to develop a way of capturing the rainfall and storing it for use in time of need through a reservoir system and a network of large and small irrigation channels. The stored water also serves important purification purposes – for personal cleanliness and to clean clothes and utensils.

For the people of the Kayah state the elements, through the metamorphoses of nature, represent the unfolding of a mystery. For these people water is synonymous with rebirth and forms part of an immense and all-important cycle. The colour red evokes the 'blood of the earth', and symbolises both the outpouring of passion and the transmigrations people must undergo. Water embodies transparency, depth, the magic of reflection, the source of fertility, but also represents a challenge to be overcome in order to reach the other side – the blessed state of nirvana.

The royal residence of King Sœ Kun Lee was built at the beginning of the century, entirely of teak. Now a Buddhist monastery, it is known as Tiri Minglaboon.

• The 'long-neck' women •

The 'long-neck' women of Burma are members of the Padaung people, a Kayin tribe, and are famous for their strange custom of wearing a spiral of bronze rings around their necks. These rings can weigh as much as 5 kg [11 lb] and cause the collarbone to be depressed.

The reason for the custom seems to have to do with Padaung mythology and its account of the origins of the tribe. According to this, man was the wind, and woman was a beautiful dragon. The original dragon-woman was impregnated by the wind to give rise to the first Padaung people. Ever since that time Padaung women have worn rings around their necks in imitation of the first dragon-mother figure. The ornamentation is not confined to the neck alone. 'Long-neck' women also wear bronze rings, or fine rings of bamboo or lacquered cord, around their wrists, ankles and knees. Their main occupation in Burma (around Loikaw) and in Thailand (near Mae Hong Son) is to pose for tourist photographs.

In the Shan state, the largest in Burma, all agricultural work is carried out manually by family groups. Women carry their babies on their backs in the fields.

The Shan state is the largest and most mountainous state in Myanmar, covering almost a quarter of the country. The river Thanlwin or Salween runs through it from north to south. To the west lie deep gorges and inaccessible peaks while to the east is the tangled mass of mountains that lead into China, Laos, and Thailand.

The Shan and other hill peoples inhabiting this area are proud and independent and have fought the central government for many years. The opium poppy, *papaver somniferum*, flourishes in the climate and soil of the region, which has become the realm of the opium barons.

The Shan, one of the Tai peoples, represent the state's largest ethnic group. Traditionally, their society had a rigid hierarchical structure. They subdivided their territory into principalities or mini-states, each one ruled over by a *sawba* or *chao fa luang*. The power of these princes was considerable, and the British were careful neither to tread on their toes, nor to compromise the independence of their princedoms. That was left to the Burmese government, which has sought to impose profound social and economic changes, triggering a long-standing, violent and bloody anti-Rangoon reaction.

Symbolism plays an important part in Shan culture, and the land itself takes on a poetical significance. The Shan people communicate with the mountains from the depth of their souls; for them the ambivalence of existential truth remains always and fundamentally allied to primordial forces. The originality of Burmese culture, and Shan culture in particular, stems from this ability to 'listen to' phenomena which, like equations, are open to interpretation on a number of different and mysterious levels. The Pindaya caves, which contain almost 8,000 statues of the Buddha, remain an enigma, as do the small, white pagodas perched on the hill and the slumbering remains of the Shwe Ohn Hmin that stand near the lake.

Here all appears to be bathed in the innermost depths of a timeless corporeality, and in order to decode this parallel reality it is important to understand that certain spiritual essences are reversible, enabling apprehension of the two extremes of a perceived reality like the two slopes of a mountain.

This sense that the Burmese, and the people of the Shan region in particular, enjoy takes the form of a dynamic reverie dissolving all and purifying the corporeal.

But it is not to see pagodas that one visits the Shan state, rather to immerse oneself in the colours of a magical force that will envelop the visitor like a cloak of light. The main tourist centre of the region is Kalaw. This peaceful town, once the haunt of British government officials, is a good starting point from which to visit the area. The Shan state is home to the Pa-O, a Karen tribe who generally dress in dark shades of black or indigo. They speak a Tibeto-Burman language and, like the Palaung, are Buddhist-animists.

Palaung women are noted for their characteristic style of dress: a full, red skirt over hoops of bamboo, a blue jacket with a red front, and a gold-coloured headdress – in honour of the gods of heaven and earth.

Following pages:
One of the main tribes living in the Shan state is the Pa-O. Like their forebears, the women wear dark clothes and colourful towelling turbans.

The floating market at Ywama is, without doubt, the most colourful in the whole of South-East Asia. The people of the Intha and Pa-O tribes come by boat from the surrounding villages once a week to trade the fish they have caught and the produce they have grown.

Following pages:

Intha fishermen on Lake Inle are known for their unusual method of rowing their boats and for their unique fishing method: moving along in the shallow waters of the lake, they methodically push their cone-shaped nets into the water whenever they suspect a fish is lurking in the vegetation covering the bottom of the lake.

Lake Inle is a vast but shallow body of water – no more than 5 metres [16 ft] deep but 22 km [14 miles] long and 11 km [7 miles] wide. It has an allure all its own; water hyacinths abound in the lake, turning it into a magical water garden. On its islands and along its shores live some 80,000 members of the Intha people, believed to have come originally from Dawei in the Tanintharyi region. The most poetic tale of the origin of this ethnic group tells how two brothers from Dawei entered the service of a local Shan chief, who was so satisfied with their work that he asked them to bring more families to the state. It is said that all Intha people are descendants of this original group. On a more historical note, it has been claimed that the Inthas are descended from a people reduced to slavery by a local potentate, or that the first Inthas came as refugees from the civil war between the Burmans and the Siamese. Intha means 'child of the lake'. The Intha people are one of the richest ethnic groups in Burma. They grow a wide range of flowers, vegetables, and fruit on islands floating in the lake. These are composed of mud and the rotting vegetation of the water hyacinths and make a very fertile growing environment.

The mining region of Mogok is the source of most of Burma's rubies. The valley is ineffectively controlled by the state army and has a dangerous reputation. For many years foreigners were excluded, but this ban is gradually being lifted and it is now possible to visit the region if you obtain a special permit.

Long ago, when the kings of Burma were still demigods and long before the Buddha brought his message to the world, an eagle soared over Burma. It was the largest eagle that had ever lived. Below it the eagle spied an enormous rock so red that at first the bird thought it was a piece of living flesh, so similar was it in colour to human blood. The bird carried the rock off and set it down on the edge of the nearest valley; thus it was that Mogok was born.

Mogok lies in the 'valley of the rubies' and is a place made legendary by the dreams of the treasure seekers who have passed through it. Perched up in the mountains at a height of 1,170 metres [3,800 ft], Mogok's main attraction is the fascination with and cult of precious stones. Of these the most highly prized are the Mogok rubies. The feverish atmosphere of this mining town has attracted a largely Asian population – Burmese, Nepalese, Sikhs, and Chinese craftsmen and merchants who make their living from precious stones such as lapis lazuli, moonstones, garnets, and chrysoberyls.

Mogok stands on the shore of a lake. Its pagodas offer a serenity that is a striking contrast to the cosmopolitan atmosphere of the main town.

Lashio, the administrative capital of the northern Shan state, is situated on the famous Burma Road. It was along this road that supplies reached Chiang Kai-shek's army in their fight against the communist troops of Mao Zedong. The Kuomintang troops were placed under the authority of the American general Joseph Warren Stilwell, commander-in-chief of the fifth and sixth Chinese nationalist armies stationed in Burma.

The Burma Road also played a major strategic role during the Second World War. When it was cut off by the Japanese, it was replaced by an airlift system between India and China.

Though closed to foreigners for many years, the town of Lashio is now open to tourists – with certain restrictions – and has become an important centre of trade between China and Burma. The town boasts the largest Chinese temple in Burma, the Guan Yin San.

Keng Tung is Burma's principal city within the Golden Triangle and is notorious for its opium traffickers. Historically the town is also the centre of the Khun culture, which is related to that of the Thais, who are ethnic brothers of the Shan. A Shan prince by the name of Mangrai played an important role in Siam as it was he who founded Chiang Mai and the Lanna kingdom, from which the Khun people originated.

Keng Tung means 'fortified town of Tung' – Tung being the mythical founder of the town – and is easily accessible to tourists arriving from the northern Thai town of Mae Sai. It is a charming and peaceful place with many Buddhist temples and old colonial buildings.

Buried deep in a valley, this village, home to the Ann tribe, seems unaltered by time.

*Ox-drawn carts await the heavily
laden fishing boats.*

*T*he fish are quickly unloaded and spread out on the beach to dry in the sun. The men do the fishing, but drying the catch is a job for the women of the village.

The state of Arakan or Rakhine is situated in the north-west of Burma and shares a border with Bangladesh and the eastern tip of India. In geographical terms the Arakan Yoma mountain range divides the Arakan and Chin states from the central Irrawaddy plain. The inhabitants of this region of Myanmar have remained culturally close to neighbouring Bengal – land and sea connections between the two areas being relatively easy.

Immigrant Tibeto-Burmans, fusing with the inhabitants of the region's early Indianized kingdoms, gave rise to the Rakhine or Arakenese ethnic group. The name Rakhine is said to derive from *rakha* (barbarous, savage) or from *raksapura* (Sanskrit for 'land of the ogres'). Presumably the immigrant pale-skinned Indo-Aryans applied this pejorative designation to the (putatively Austroasiatic) aboriginals, whose dark skin, frizzy hair and neolithic culture made a deep impression on the first Buddhist missionaries.

It is thought that these first kingdoms were established in the second century, continuing undisturbed until the arrival of the famous Pyu – tribes of Tibeto-Burman origin. The Pyu took power but soon came under the control of the kings of Bagan and then the Sultanate of Bengal. This saw the spread of Islam or, to be more precise, of Muslim culture with its mathematics and science. The Rakhine rulers, though Buddhist, held an Islamic title.

The most powerful dynasty founded the town of Mrauk-U which, for nearly three centuries, ruled over an entire kingdom frequented not only by Arab and Asian merchants but by others from further afield such as Denmark, Holland, and Portugal. Mrauk-U was an international crossroads of such economic and political power that it was able to overcome Rangoon and even Bago, which was conquered in 1663 by the Rakhine king Razagyi. However, the system instituted by the king did not succeed in integrating all the different elements making up his new territory; pirates and local potentates in particular refused to yield, and the collapse of the kingdom was the result of resistance by the latter. It was reconquered by the Burmese in 1784, before being taken over by the British in 1826.

Today the inhabitants of Arakan make their living from the sea and from rice cultivation. The south of the region is famous for its immaculate beaches, once frequented by British government officials. They are among the finest beaches in South-East Asia. The most popular is the Ngapoli beach, whose name, according to some locals, is derived from the Italian Napoli. The story goes that an Italian living in the place so missed the Bay of Naples that he asked the local authorities to christen the beach in its honour. However, others will tell you that in Burmese Ngapoli means 'cajoling fish'. Ngapoli beach is over 3 km [nearly 2 miles] long and during the monsoon season from May to September offers excellent surf, attracting large numbers of surfing enthusiasts.

Thandwe, 10 km [6 miles] to the north-east is a port of call between India and Malaysia. According to Buddhist tradition the Buddha spent three of his 547 previous lives in this small town, where three hill shrines were erected during the eighth century. The Andaw Pagoda enshrines one of the Buddha's molars, the Nandaw Pagoda one of his ribs, and the Sandow Pagoda a strand of his hair.

*F*ollowing pages:
The medieval capital of the Arakan lies 80 km [50 miles] from the mouth of the river Kaladan. The site, built by King Minsawmun, can be reached by boat. The journey takes 6 hours.
The temples at Mrauk-U, though less well known than those at Pagan, have their own special charm. The Shitthaung shrine, known as the temple of the 80,000 Buddhas, dominates the whole site.

Sittwe or Akyab is the provincial capital of North Arakan and lies at the mouth of the 348 km [215 mile] long Kaladan river, which provides access to the region's interior. Geographically Sittwe is an important transit point and has been inhabited for two thousand years. During the colonial period the British made great use of the city, and the nineteenth century saw a thriving international trade along this stretch of coast.

Historically North Arakan enjoyed political renown, particularly during the reign of King Tiri-Thu-Dhama. This monarch is notorious for the 'elixir of immortality' prepared for him using the hearts of 2,000 white doves, 4,000 white cows, and 6,000 human beings. The king died nevertheless – poisoned by his courtiers.

His successor, who depended for his power on the support of Portuguese pirates in his paid service, suffered some serious setbacks. The Moghul governor of Bengal bought these pirates over and they then turned against their former master. During the eighteenth century North Arakan descended into anarchy, a situation of which the British took advantage.

Today all that remains of the region's former glory is a handful of temples and ruins. Nearby are small country villages, and sometimes in the evening the strains of an old Burmese song can be heard. It speaks of the impossibility of species existing side by side without each bringing about the eternal destruction of the other; it tells of the need for people to give fresh life to them from within their own being and to lead them to the shore of the reservoir where once the floodgates would have been opened to drown their enemy.

Unconcerned by the remarkable archaeological sites that surround them, the villagers of Mrauk-U go peacefully about their daily chores, driving their ox carts past the Ratanabon chedi or pagoda and in the evening washing by the Ley-Myet-Na Temple.